From ISO to POS – Point of Sale from the Makers of Exatouch®

From ISO to POS – Point of Sale from the Makers of Exatouch®

By

Terry L. Glatt

Exatouch Publishing

International Standard Book Number: 978-0615905594

Updated November 2014

exatouch.com

To my beautiful wife and amazing son …
Thanks for your patience and support!

Contents

Introduction

From ISO to POS is intended to help lay a knowledge foundation for a consultative approach to selling point of sale equipment (POS) for ISOs. Merchant processing independent sales organizations (ISOs) are in a unique position to profit from the POS revolution. There was a time, very recently in fact, when smartphones were for early adopters and techies. The market plowed right through that condition with the help of price reduction, feature pull from users, proliferation of apps, and ease of use. Point of sale equipment is set to really explode for small retailers for a very similar set of reasons. ISOs can readily adapt their sales channels from merchant processing sales to POS sales, without a lot of investment. In fact ISOs are uniquely positioned to drive POS to the market for contract services, much like the cell phone model.

Like smart phones, POS until recently has been for the early adopters. The only small retailers with POS systems are the tech savvy or very successful. Like early cell phones, the features and functions are narrow in scope. POS is in a position to really grow as more and more functionality finds its way into systems like Exatouch; much like apps did for smartphones.

POS has a very loose definition and sometimes includes devices like iPads running apps, credit card machines, and full-blown commercial grade big-box systems. This book will attempt to shed light on and help with an understanding of all of the above. The focus will be on selling Exatouch, as that unapologetically is our product. The approach will be knowledge-based sales ... communicating the benefits of POS to retailer customers.

Each chapter presents a different subject as it pertains to selling POS, from the perspective of an ISO and its agents. Some redundancy may be noticed in that some information is germane to more than one section. The author hopes From ISO to POS becomes a sort of handbook for the ISO sales agents who want to capitalize on the impending POS boom. Further I hope you will find Exatouch a worthy partner in this POS journey you are about to take.

Chapter 1 – Transition to POS

The Merchant processing independent sales organizations (ISOs) are seeing their businesses change, and not for the better. Point of sale is their future. Let's face it there isn't a much less exciting product to sell than a credit card machine and merchant account. What used to be a great money maker is now a commodity. Many times it is recognized as an expense, since the merchant knows it skims off a percentage of profit every time they use it. The credit card machine just sits there on the counter waiting to be fed.

It's getting harder and harder to compete on a few basis points and "great service". The best you can do is highlight the increase in revenue from taking credit cards and the fantastic care and customer service you as their ISO can give the merchant.

While the residuals can make it worthwhile, merchant account sales has become a real challenge, especially with interchange pass through and free equipment the norm. Your business is facing demise and those who don't take action won't survive.

An agent's personal satisfaction from a merchant sale is almost non-existent. While the residual is the agent's primary motivator, most sales people would like to enjoy what they do and like to be satisfied in the process.

Selling point of sale is an almost entirely different type of sale. POS is a consultative sale, whereas a simple merchant account is more of a commodity sale. POS is assuredly the future of payments processing sales.

Successful POS selling will reward the agent in at least five new ways, the five 'R's:

1. Rebirth: Your business will be born again. Commodity margin squeeze, as with any mature market, GONE. POS is a whole new basis for differentiating your business to your merchants. You won't have to be the lowest in rates, good rates, but not necessarily the lowest. With a POS system like Exatouch, leasing revenue is back! That's right, with a POS system that you provide with hardware, you can lease again. Note: leasing is not usually an option for software-only POS.

2. Retention: POS is sticky; merchants will stay. Attrition goes to single digits. POS is much more important to the merchant's business. Merchants touch their POS 1000+ times a day. Once it's running their business, you'll have to really screw up to lose them.

3. <u>Residuals</u>: Businesses that run on POS typically realize significant improvement in revenue due to many benefits like efficiency and cost reduction, loss reduction, marketing, and customer satisfaction.

4. <u>Rewarding</u>: For the inclined ISO agent, the consultative sale of POS is a very personally rewarding improvement in their life. With the right system like Exatouch, your merchants will view you as a great help, a partner who has set them up for properly managing their business for success. This relationship will prove to be very rewarding.

5. <u>Referrals</u>: Success breeds success. Your happy POS merchant lives in a community and will certainly know other business owners. They will always refer their POS consultant and system when they have a chance.

Remember the 5 'R's:

1.   Rebirth,
2.   Retention,
3.   Residuals,
4.   Rewarding,
5.   Referrals.

These are the core of your transition from ISO to POS.

On top of it all, small retail is likely the most technically under-served market in the world. Think about it, your house likely has far more technology than most small businesses. Some retailers actually still play music on compact disc. ISOs are perfectly positioned to capitalize!

Chapter 2 – ISO Sales Program

Making it easy for the ISO too …

With Exatouch POS, ISOs should seriously consider an offer much like mobile phones and cable television. All the cell phone service providers offer their phones at subsidized pricing to the users in return for service contracts. These contracts commit the users to the service provider with early termination fees.

As published on Harbortouch.com, an early mover in the ISO POS transition, an ISO can consider offering an POS system for "free" with a merchant account and a monthly support fee and agreement for four years. Depending on the business model developed, an ISO could offer $89, $99, $109 a month with subsidy, or with a lease. The payback for the subsidized model can be shown to approach 8 to 14 months, depending on the account[1]. With the Exatouch patent pending ISO Lock-Down Module, this business model should be a serious consideration for ISOs transitioning to POS.

In most cases, good service means a customer for a long, long time. There is a good bit of churn, but the turnover is almost

---

[1] Contact XTT to learn more about this business model.

always due to poor service. Exatouch POS is an opportunity for ISOs to subsidize their merchants for POS systems and lock them in for very lucrative and lasting merchant services contracts, just like cell phones, cable, satellite, even alarm systems. It's all about locking in that service contract. A commitment to good service and competitive rates is important for success, as is the selection of an effective POS product like Exatouch and supportive partner like XTT.

Merchant processing sales agents are fantastic sales people by definition, payments is a tough sell these days and anyone making a living do so is very talented. Armed with the right knowledge, approach, and offer, transitioning ISO agents to POS will be productive. The 5 Rs above will make it worthwhile.

There are two very effective ISO programs to sell Point of Sale:
1. Data Mining, and
2. Appointment setting.
As an ISO transitioning to POS, your goal is to ensure a low cost of acquisition and make the most of the lead sources and sales resources you already have.

Both of the following programs will benefit from representative and agent training guided by this book.

Program 1, Data Mining:

Mine your current data and identify which merchants would be a potential fit for a POS system. Two things to look at are merchant type (retail, restaurant, etc.) and what type of technology they are currently using. Businesses using a credit card terminal or computer gateway are perfect candidates for point of sale. Any merchant that does not have POS will likely have a system within the next 5 years, it is your job to ensure it comes from you!

Once you have identified a merchant candidate, use a newly trained outbound sales team to call and convert them. This is a very inexpensive way to gain top line revenue (leasing?) and reduce attrition by locking them in with POS. Further, software like the Exatouch patent-pending lock down feature prevents the software from operating with a merchant account other than from the ISO from which it was purchased.

This is great way to reduce attrition and improve your profitability through your current satisfied and loyal customer base!

Program 2, Appointment Setting:

Convert your existing new-merchant appointment setting process to POS. Here, your scripts need to lead with your POS offering ... merchant processing all but disappears from the conversation. The scripts and approach should be laced with the benefits and advantages for the merchant, as well as the value of your offer, which only an ISO can bring.

The good news is that merchants will be a very receptive audience. First, it is highly likely they know about and even want POS, if they don't already have it. Second, they will be very familiar with getting a cell phone at a reduced price in lieu of a service commitment, and know the benefit. Even if they are leasing, the monthly payment should easily fit their budget. In fact, you'll be happy with the pricing for Exatouch POS and how easily it will fit into a small retailer's budget.

POS provides the ISO team a substantial advantage over its competition in two ways, 1. POS makes the agent a consultant, a partner if you will, to the merchant ... with a high-value offering and 2. POS is a passive way to win merchant processing accounts.

Outside agents need a sticky sales advantage that will help them close sales in the ever competitive merchant processing space. POS like Exatouch provides that advantage, stickiness, and long-term customer loyalty.

Example Script

"Good afternoon, this is Linda with ISO Payments. We are calling to give you the opportunity to upgrade the technology that runs your business with a point of sale system you probably heard about, Exatouch; quite possibly for free.

Not all merchants qualify for our offer, so I have a couple of questions to qualify you, in just one minute.

Do you currently have a point of sale system or do you run on a cash register?

POS → *When did you purchase your point of sale system? Most owners express challenges with their current point of sale.*

NO POS → *Boy, I'm sure you're familiar with POS systems. What has prevented you from running on POS?*

\<gather info\>

As I mentioned, I'm with ISO Payments and we have cutting edge technology for our merchants. And our offer works a lot like how you got your cell phone.

Exatouch is a full-featured point of sale that saves you time and money, and in fact very quickly pays for itself, and then makes you money. The stand-alone robust Atom comes with everything included and the PADie is for merchants looking for a tablet POS.

We've developed the ability to provide you with our POS systems very affordably, maybe even free.

Since I've called you out of the blue, I don't want to take any more of your time right now. I would like to schedule some time with you where we can discuss this offer in more detail, maybe even come in and show you Exatouch in person at no charge. Do you have some time on your calendar next week?

<set appointment>"

Chapter 3 – Sales Approach

ISO sales agents have great sales chops. Disenchantment and challenge may be increasing due to margin squeeze and having little to compete with. POS to the rescue!

Energize your sales team with high demand, high growth POS products to sell. POS can be very exciting for the right agent scenario. Not only will it be refreshing to sell something differentiating, but the merchants will be easier to retain, not lost to another ISO for a few basis points and a free machine.

POS is sticky because it runs the merchant's business … all their clients, inventory, reporting, even marketing is in the system. POS merchants are known to be much less likely to leave. A good POS like Exatouch can reduce attrition to single digits.

Messaging

The following are not necessarily for verbatim use, but as messaging examples to be adopted to your approach, perhaps as openers.

"I can offer you a very low price on a POS system, much the same way the price was low for your cell phone."

"We want your merchant account, and much like your cell phone, we can do the same to the price for a full featured POS system for your shop."

"Have you considered a point of sale system for your shop? We have a new and unique program to get you one almost free."

"Have you seen the offer for free POS systems? Well we all know nothing is free, but I can get you awfully close."

"I can show you a POS system you can easily afford that will go ever farther and pay for itself immediately."

"On a scale of paper to Wal-Mart®, where do you want your business to operate? Your big competitors have POS."

"Most of your competitors will be running more efficiently on a POS system. I have one to offer that is extremely affordable."

"I know how much time you spend closing up each day. We have a very affordable POS system that can save you a lot of time. Not just on closing out, but many other ways too."

"Have you thought about how a good POS system will help you manage and grow your business? I have a system you can easily fit into your budget."

How Exatouch POS pays for itself

- Business value – "Your business will be worth more with a professional POS system. Its value will be easy to see."

- Marketing – "One or two additional sales from the marketing module can pay for the system alone, e.g. birthday emails."

- Time Savings – "What is your time worth? Clearly it's worth a lot. The time saved by not needing to z or batch out each night, the tax-time convenience of POS reporting, email reports ... these, and others, will pay for the system immediately."

- Loss prevention – "POS systems act as a sort of watch dog. While not surveillance per se, staff-based loss is known to be reduced due to the transaction and inventory control of a POS system in the store."

- Customer service – "Fast ring-ups, inventory accuracy, Exatouch programmable gift certificates, and messaging all improve customer service and increase sales."

- Purchasing – "Having the right inventory when you need it prevents lost sales. Low inventory alerts and PO creation can help."
- Staff efficiency – "A good POS system not only helps with managing your staff, but make them much more efficient in their tasks … saving you money."

Growth/Future

"Your business' growth and future depend on having a good POS system; you can't operate on paper and a cash register and expect to grow your business."

Demos

An ISO should have a demonstrator unit. If the unit is portable, a travel case is recommended. Your POS partner should be able to provide sources for a good travel case. XTT can provide this information for Exatouch partners. Note that there is a free demo version of Exatouch available to partners.

A very effective way to demonstrate the system is through screen sharing software, like join.me on the web. Here, you can run the POS and a prospect merchant can log in and see the actual product working, driven by their ISO agent. Again, the ISO's POS partner can help the ISO in setting up their screen sharing capability for demonstrating the product.

Chapter 4 – Advantages

User Advantages

Easy to use – Keep in mind, POS is miles from a credit card machine. The credit card machine sits behind the counter and is touched for a few seconds every once in a while. POS on the other hand is touched a thousand times a day. The business truly depends on its POS, which is actually a small business management system.

Exatouch POS is designed for touch screen, from scratch, with ease of use as the top priority. The system is designed with the small retailer in mind, not typically the most tech savvy, but talented in their craft … enough to own a business. Exatouch is easy to use, yet, the savvy user can go deep when they want.

Great support – Help is there where you need it. Facebook, Twitter, texts, web, email, phone … XTT wants the user to have the best experience. We represent the ISO *and* Exatouch to be sure the merchant is happy with their decision to run on Exatouch POS.

Accountability – Another merchant-user advantage with Exatouch is the dual accountability that comes with ISO involvement. It's just like both Apple®'s and AT&T®'s vested interest in the iPhone. They both want the iPhone user to be thrilled so they keep using the AT&T cell service on iPhones. Ditto for Exatouch ... Exatouch and the ISO will keep each other accountable for a good merchant experience. Advantage – merchant.

Great features – For example, SideKick PADie ... here a PADie works as a SideKick to an Atom. The SideKick is then in-store mobile and can be taken out on the floor for great customer service. This is big-box stuff you only usually see in the Apple store for example. Exatouch brings this capability to SMB retailers.

Another example is Matrix Inventory ... retailers know what this is. Matrix is where an item like a shirt comes in with a variety of sizes and colors (a matrix of size and color) but under one factory SKU. Exatouch manages this for the retailer and in fact assigns a local SKU and tracks the Matrix items by both SKUs. Nice feature.

Check the features chapter to learn more about Exatouch features.

Affordable – The system pays for itself. This is clear and easy to point out; efficiency, time savings, loss reduction, and marketing. For the progressive thinking ISO, Exatouch may even be free to the merchant. This would be a subsidy scenario, much like cell providers give away their phones for service contracts. The forward-thinking ISO could easily do the same. Harbortouch$^{®}$ is one example that does.

See the Sales Approach chapter for further information on how Exatouch POS easily pays for itself.

ISO Advantages

Keep residuals – Unlike many POS solutions, Exatouch does not revenue-share the residuals. The ISO can adopt Exatouch as its in-house POS solution knowing that their business model is preserved.

Easy to sell – Exatouch POS is designed to be easy for everyone. Especially easy for ISOs, the products are fully supported by XTT, letting the ISO focus on what they do best. The merchant benefits are easy to communicate and the pricing is very easy on the budget. ISO subsidy can really make it easy for the merchant to say yes.

ISO Lock Down – Since the systems are sold by the ISO, Exatouch's patent applied for ISO Lock Down ensures the systems sold by an ISO are locked to that ISO … in a similar way to how AT&T iPhones are locked to AT&T.

Leasing revenue – Exatouch is eligible for leasing. Since the system is software *and* hardware, Exatouch brings leasing back!

Mine existing merchants – Exatouch POS enables ISOs to mine their existing merchants to provide POS to them for increasing revenue, but perhaps more valuable, decreasing attrition. POS merchants stick around.

Sales support – Exatouch provides sales support to ISOs. Webinars, demos, sales sheets, personalized web site, and phone support are all available to ISOs and their agents, to assist with selling Exatouch POS.

PCI – Exatouch is listed on the PCI PA-DSS validated payment applications web page.

No gateway – ISOs board directly to the acquirer. No gateway fees to pay.

POS Marketplace is Very Fragmented

The POS market has a number of players but a number of them are only partial solutions. Even the big boys like Microsoft® and QuickBooks® struggled in POS. Not many have it right yet. Just like Apple® solved the digital music problem with iTunes® and the iPod®, Exatouch® has for POS. Nicely integrated software, hardware, and services in an easy to setup, easy to use, and easy to own form factor with great support (for the user *and* ISO).

Chapter 5 – Objections and Tidbits

Selling POS is a big change from selling the past and "current" payment technology.   It's no longer as easy as offering discounted rates and free equipment.   Merchants are skeptical and nervous when it comes to change and spending. Understanding your customer, knowing POS, and learning how to deal with objections is the key to winning the merchant's confidence, and the sale.

The most likely objection is **cost**.   Although POS can realistically range from $1800 to $8000, it can be offered with many different payment options to alleviate the large upfront expense.   Overcoming the price objection comes down to showing how the purchase will pay for itself in short order. This fast payback is realized through managing the business more effectively, increasing top line revenue e.g. email marketing, and controlling expenses at the touch of a button. Depending on how effectively the merchant embraces the benefits of POS, their business will benefit, as shown in the table below:

	HIGH EFFICIENCY GAIN	MEDIUM EFFICIENCY GAIN	MODERATE EFFICIENCY GAIN
SALES INCREASE	+20%	+10%	+5%
EXPENSE DECREASE	-15%	-8%	-2%
MARGIN INCREASE	+25%	+15%	+5%
NET PROFIT INCREASE	+30%	+12%	+3%

Table 1 Benefits of Point of Sale for Small Business

Startup Budget

Many retailers don't have a POS system in their startup budget as they don't think it's affordable. The ISO POS agent can quickly justify the cost and show how the system actually saves, even makes, the merchant money. They'll get more accomplished with fewer employees, many tasks are automated by the system.

A Good POS System is Very Cost Effective

Affordable support including free upgrades, equipment coverage and of course caring support. All the above available with Exatouch makes it very cost-effective. Also, doing more with fewer staff and higher efficiency saves money for the merchant. Accountants love retailers who run on POS, they hate a shoe box full of paper at tax time! Their job is much easier with reporting, and accountants can be expensive.

Owner is Not a Techie or a Biz Wiz

Another objection is **difficulty** of use and the time it will take management and staff to be effective on a POS system.

A merchant quite possibly needs help learning how to make money with their business. Exatouch POS brings it all together … shop management, marketing, inventory control, reporting; it's like an MBA in a box!

Training is key in the effective use of POS and how that translates to operating an effective business. However, an easy-to-use system goes a very long way. Sometimes staff turnover is high and an easy system to learn and good training is invaluable in getting new staff up and productive. There is a full spectrum of use models in the POS space and it's important to choose an easy-to-use and intuitive system like Exatouch. Be careful with finicky apps and legacy Mouse software simply connected to a touch screen. A wise POS choice here will overcome this objection easily.

Initial training should always be provided, preferably by the point of sale provider. Inset tutorials in the software and on the web, and ongoing helpful customer care should be demonstrably available to overcome this objection. An interesting statistic shows that once all employees are fully up to speed, administrative labor costs decrease fifteen to twenty hours per week, based on the volume of the merchant.

Performance increases include: quicker checkout, faster credit card approvals, accuracy of checkout, print out of gift certificates, capture of customer information, accurate time clock, management of inventory, quick generation of reports … all of which highlight the payback of a POS system. With a good POS like Exatouch, retailers can run their business like a pro; even with no real computer experience.

In-Store vs. Cloud-Based vs. Cloud-Hybrid

With everyone running to the cloud it seems to be the sexy answer to most all items related to software and technology.

The cloud is effective for reporting purposes and general oversight of your systems. The downside is that the business owner does not control their data, cannot transport their data, and when their internet connectivity is lost, so is the total use of their system.

In-store is more robust, where the business owner controls their data, stays operational when internet connectivity is lost, and can effectively use their data to best manage and grow their business, and provide good customer service.

In-store systems that *also* make smart use of the Cloud are the best all-around answer. These **Cloud-Hybrid** systems, like Exatouch, are able to provide the best of both worlds to the merchant. Robust on-site technology for performance and safe-keeping, and smart use of the Cloud for availability, monitoring, backup, and flexibility.

Inventory can be a Pain

Many retailers buy from many vendors and have hundreds of items. Some have to manage seasonal inventory. Inventory is not easy. Understocking and overstocking are both bad. Inventory is much easier with a full-feature POS solution like Exatouch. Purchase orders, receiving, generate and print barcodes and labels, low level alerts, and reports ... all make this job much more effective.

Data Input may originate from existing systems, spreadsheets and paper. If formatted correctly using the provided Excel template, all data can be uploaded through a thumb drive directly into the system. Once the data is uploaded it quickly populates the system and is ready to use in minutes.

Busy Stores Need Fast Checkout

With the right POS, ring-ups go from minutes to seconds. Easy button-built orders, barcode scanning, and even comprehensive search make checkout a breeze. Add promotions and discounts, track customers, and mix payments too. Saving orders, for later checkout, and refunds are both managed quickly and easily.   There is a significant improvement in operating efficiency, saving time and money.

Chapter 6 – Benefits

Automating a small retail business has benefits that easily justify the cost of doing so. In fact the time savings alone pays for the system in short order. However, today, the majority of small retailers do not have POS and too many run on a cash register and credit card machine. It's clear that in the near future, POS penetration into the market will claim a majority. Here are some of the benefits of POS, which should be very easy to sell.

Business value – Which business would you rather buy, the store that runs on a paper, a shoe box, and a cash register, or, a store that has a POS system with accurate sales reports for any period, inventory control, and all the customers managed and accounted for in a database you can protect? POS has a direct impact on the perceived and, in fact, actual value of a business.

Business value is important not only at the time of sale of the business, but also if financing is ever sought.

Accounting – Accountants cringe when they see the shoe box come in. Ask any accountant, they don't want to be bookkeepers. Accountants love POS systems that keep accurate transactions and can report anytime for any period.

Systems like Exatouch enable regularly scheduled reports to be sent to the merchant and her accountant via email in pdf or Excel format. Accountants love this feature.

Exatouch also exports to .csv (comma separated values), a popular file format for import to accounting software like QuickBooks® and also in Excel®.

Time savings – What a time saver! Exatouch POS requires no z-out, like a cash register, and no batch out either, like a credit card terminal. Simply lock the door and go home. The merchant's transactions are batched out automatically.

Other time saving features are inventory checks, ordering items, receiving items, managing matrix items like colors and sizes, printing labels, and more.

Convenience – The convenience of having business data at your fingertips is powerful. Uncertainty has always been the nemesis of an entrepreneur. Your merchant/business owner is no stranger to the fear uncertainty creates. Managing their business on a POS system like Exatouch mitigates a lot of uncertainty for them. With complete and flexible reporting and data control at their convenience, the uncertainty is greatly reduced. Compare this to running their business on paper and a cash register and this benefit is obvious.

Accuracy—Errors cost money. Human errors especially. Exatouch POS reduces errors and saves money. Errors in transactions and inventory are especially costly. Accuracy is another benefit of POS.

Purchasing/Ordering – Exatouch POS, as any other full-featured POS should, provides a purchasing, PO, and receiving module. The Purchasing module allows for emailing POs to vendors and then receiving the inventory against a PO. Partial receiving is available as is barcode printing when received. Merchants also have the ability to receive goods NOT ordered on a PO and print labels on the spot. This is a nice feature for many retailers who come back with special purchases that were not anticipated with a purchase order. The benefit here is current, accurate, and available inventory to support sales and customer service.

Customer service – A good POS management system in a retail store brings improved customer service. Probably the most important is speedy and accurate ring-ups. Next would be gift certificates, gift cards, and loyalty programs managed through the POS system. The Exatouch PADie working out on the shop floor offers inventory checks, transactions with emailed receipts, and customer data capture for specials and promotions.

Marketing – Exatouch POS has an available marketing module where your merchant can text and email promotions to their customers, for example birthday specials.

Impression – A business running on paper and a cash register simply does not make a good impression. Consumers, especially these days, like to know they are in good hands. A technology POS solution like Exatouch gives the immediate impression of professionalism. Especially impressive is a solid POS system like Atom behind the counter and a PADie out on the floor for customer service.

Loss prevention – Loss is big part of retail. Running a business on paper and a cash register is a sure recipe for loss, if the business has employees. A good POS system is a great theft deterrent. Sweet-hearting is where an employee helps a friend with bypassing ring-up for all or part of a purchase. Employee theft is greatly deterred when the employees know there is a system tracking inventory and transactions accurately. The loss prevention benefit alone can pay for the POS system very quickly.

Exatouch partners will be able to offer additional loss prevention features in the future on Exatouch systems. Video monitoring and asset tagging are just two examples.

Chapter 7 – PCI and Security

The card issuers mandate validation of all payment application against the PCI Payment Application – Data Security Standard (PA-DSS). This means, in order for a merchant site to be PCI-DSS compliant, any payment application they use in the store must be PA-DSS validated. A payment application is *any software that touches credit card data, regardless of encryption*, including just transmitting the data. The only way a payment application is validated is through a PCI Qualified Security Assessor. Encryption may help with validation, but it still must be validated. Encryption does not obviate the need for validation. The only authority on PA-DSS is the PCI at pcisecuritystandards.org. If an application is not listed there, it is not validated.

Note that the PCI-DSS certificate for a payment gateway DOES NOT carry down to a merchant store that uses the gateway. Each merchant location is mandated to be PCI-DSS compliant on its own. That means an 'app' that uses a PCI-DSS compliant gateway is NOT PCI compliant ... unless the app is PA-DSS validated.

iPad and Android apps, at the time of this writing, are *ineligible* for PCI PA-DSS validation for secure transactions, and therefore CANNOT BE PCI compliant. Despite surprising success with inaccurate claims that a gateway's PCI-DSS server site compliance somehow translates to a merchant's business site, this is not the case. Your author is genuinely perplexed at how pervasive iOS and Android payment applications are. Until they are listed on the PCI site as validated, they are not. Be aware of your recommendations to your merchants, and remaining aware of developments at PCI will help you in your new role as a consultant to your merchants. Consider recommending only PCI validated solutions.

Exatouch is PCI PA-DSS validated.

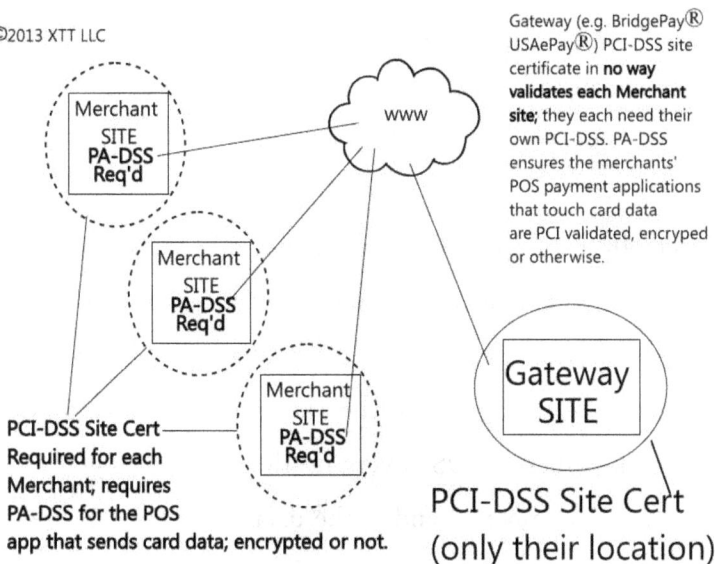

©2013 XTT LLC

Merchant SITE PA-DSS Req'd

www

Merchant SITE PA-DSS Req'd

Merchant SITE PA-DSS Req'd

Gateway (e.g. BridgePay® USAePay®) PCI-DSS site certificate in **no way validates each Merchant site**; they each need their own PCI-DSS. PA-DSS ensures the merchants' POS payment applications that touch card data are PCI validated, encryped or otherwise.

Gateway SITE

PCI-DSS Site Cert Required for each Merchant; requires PA-DSS for the POS app that sends card data; encrypted or not.

PCI-DSS Site Cert (only their location)

From ISO to POS – Point of Sale from the Makers of Exatouch

Chapter 8 – The Cloud

The "Cloud" is what's on the other side of the Internet. It means the servers and their services you connect to when you go on line. To be cloud-based means that the heavy lifting is all done on those servers via those services and the Internet.

A simple example would be a cloud-based calculator. If we wanted to add 2 + 3 on a regular calculator, you would type in 2 + 3 and get 5, all performed right on the calculator in front of you. With a cloud-based calculator you have to send the number 2, the number 3, and the operation "add" through your calculator "app" to the service running on the server in the cloud, tell it to execute the operation and send back the answer 5 to your app to display after the equals sign. The app isn't doing any of the work per se, other than transmitting and receiving requests and results respectively.

Our cloud-based calculator app may be a good answer, as long as the Internet connection is good, the web server and services are up, and you have a valid subscription to the calculator service. If any of this is not true, then your app is dead in the water. Cloud-based POS is very nearly exactly this, but a step more … the numbers 2 and 3, the data, are also in the cloud. So if you scan an item, the app sends the UPC number to the cloud service, but only the web server "knows" what the number means, what the item is, what the price is, are there any in stock, etc. If the Internet is down, or the web server is down, or you cancel your subscription, the app is worthless and the data stays in the cloud.

The author believes in the cloud for many good reasons, but subscribe to the sound information technology theory that mission critical applications should not depend on the cloud.

Smart use of the cloud, or Cloud-Hybrid is the Exatouch approach. CloudOverSite™ for example, uses the cloud to remotely monitor a business. Cloud backup puts a backup of the data up in the cloud in case of data loss, but the mission critical data processing and storage is in-store. Most smart business owners will feel much more comfortable with this scenario. Using the on-site stability in harmony with smart use of the Cloud provides a true professional's solution to run a business.

It will be a long time, if ever, before Wal-Mart® or Best Buy™ go totally cloud-based; though they clearly use the cloud in very smart ways otherwise, just like Exatouch.

Not even Apple stores run cloud-based … they run their iPads and iPod Touches in "SideKick" mode via Wi-Fi on the network.

Chapter 9 – Features

Highlighted Exatouch Features (some optional)

- Great user support

- Great ISO (sales) support

- Easy data input

- SideKick/PADie

- Backup USB *and* Cloud

- CloudOverSite™ cloud-hybrid technology

- Remote access

- Built in programmable Gift Certificates

- Remote support

- Mixed payments

- Multiple merchant accounts

- Matrix Inventory

- Bulk Product Management

- Export data to bookkeeping (e.g. QuickBooks®)

- Multi-location gift cards

- Fantastic schedule, e.g. salon or other service business

- Table map

- Remote printers (e.g. kitchen, bar)

- Sell by fraction with integrated scale support

General Product Features

The following general features are part of the Exatouch POS system.

Easy Data Entry

Data entry is as easy as possible with Exatouch. First, the system defines an easy minimal set of required data to get going. While the system will track a lot of information about items, not all of it is necessary to be productive with the system.

The system works with an on screen keyboard or a plug in keyboard. There is a preference setting so you can determine if the keyboard appears when you touch a data field once, or twice.

The system remembers previously entered values, e.g. the area code for phone numbers. This is a smart feature that assumes a lot of reuse of area codes and other data like city, zip codes, sizes, etc.

UPC numbers are the numbers on products represented by their barcodes. Merchants can simply scan a product's UPC to enter the number in the database.

Data Import

Exatouch publishes an Excel template for importing data to the system. So, if a previous POS allowed the export of data, as does Exatouch, the merchant can "massage" the export based on the import template for easy import into the system. Once the data is in template form, import is done at the touch of a button. Exatouch also offers data import as a service which can be resold by ISOs.

Internet Connection

Exatouch systems are Internet connected. The web connection is used for transactions, Cloud-Oversite™ remote access, online backup, remote support, messaging and marketing, and in the future web store management.

Backups

Backups are critical to any computer usage. Applications and programs are typically not backed up as they are readily reinstalled. However, data backups are crucial. Just ask anyone who suffered a crash or other loss of data from theft, fire, or error. Data loss is a sinking feeling that is easily fixed with a recent backup restore.

Exatouch provides easy backup to a USB drive (unlike iPad POS which has no USB). This feature is an important one to merchants … they can rest assured their data is safe in hand, and it's their data. Contrast this to running in "the Cloud" where the data is the Cloud's and if the merchant leaves the service, they leave their data behind.

Smart use of the Cloud *is* a feature. While Exatouch data is in-store, Exatouch offers an optional Cloud backup, or on-line backup. This is a great feature to ensure regular off-site backups as recommended by any good IT person.

Remote support

Exatouch Help can access the machine remotely, as long as the user has enabled Remote Support. This feature allows the merchant to get help live on the screen, as if the Help representative was in the store. Nearly all functions can be accessed while the user is watching. Remote Support is a great comfort for merchants and a fantastic training tool as well.

Remote Access – CloudOverSite™

CloudOverSite is an option that allows the authorized user (e.g. owner) access to their Exatouch eco-system. This feature is implemented over a secure Internet connection with multiple levels of password protection and security. CloudOverSite is a great way for owners to check in and monitor their store, conduct business off-site, and their system is always "aware".

Training Mode

Exatouch POS includes a feature to switch the entire data base to a "sandbox" database for training purposes. This is a smart feature not available in most POS systems. New staff and users can be in training mode and leave no impact on the real data of the business.

Transactions – Cash Register

The primary feature of a POS system is streamlining flexible transactions. Exatouch provides a full-featured cash register module managed in three pages:

1. Composer,
2. Order Details,
3. Payment.

The Composer is a finger-button driven order builder. This is a fast and easy way to ring-up transactions. The Composer includes buttons for a fast credit or cash transaction.

Order Details allows the user to manipulate the order. For example: add a customer, add a discount or promotion, change the sell price, assign staff, sell a gift certificate or miscellaneous item.

Payment is where the order is paid for. This page allows for mixed payments, for example some on a credit card and some cash. Here is where the cashier can redeem a gift certificate or gift card or take a (PIN) debit card too.

Exatouch has implemented a smart cash register. For example, BOGO discounts are automatically applied.

The Register has an on-screen number pad and the whole system is designed finger-friendly from the start, unlike many POS mouse systems running on a touch screen.

Cash Drawer

Every Exatouch Atom™ and XT come with a cash drawer. The cash drawer is optional for PADie. The cash drawer automatically opens upon completion of a transaction. There is a convenient preference for not opening the drawer for credit-only transactions where the slips can be put in the drawer through the front slot.

Bank Management

Bank management is optional and allows the user to open a bank, make adjustments, and balance the bank at the end of a shift. Multiple banks can be managed at once and assigned to different staff.

Multiple Merchant Accounts (MIDs)

A nice feature of advanced POS systems, such as Exatouch, is support of multiple merchant accounts. This functionality is important in examples like renter salons. Here, each stylist is a "chair renter" and may in fact want their own merchant account.

Inventory Management

Exatouch, as with any full POS system, provides complete inventory management. From item data input and importing to transactions, reporting, and purchasing and receiving, it's all about buying, selling, and tracking product. Following are some of the highlights of the POS inventory module.

Categories/Subcategories

Exatouch allows the merchant to assign a category and subcategory to items to facilitate transactions and reporting.

User Fields

There are three user-definable fields that can be used for reporting. For example, one User Field could be material for jewelry and the values might be gold, silver, plastic, stone, etc.

Labels

Item labels can be printed and applied, barcodes included.

Barcodes and Local UPC

Barcodes are based on UPC numbers and Exatouch allows for locally generated UPC/SKU numbers and barcodes. This is very useful where in many cases, e.g. crafts, items do not have a UPC from the manufacturer. The optional barcode scanner is required to scan barcodes, but the UPC number generator is included.

Matrix Inventory

Matrix Inventory is a feature reserved for only the higher-end POS systems. Exatouch supports matrix inventory. This feature is very handy for boutiques, shoe stores, and the like where a single manufacturer UPC could cover multiple sizes and colors of an item. Many light duty POS systems, like App POS systems cannot manage this scenario. For example, a golf shirt that is ordered under one UPC but comes in a box with an assortment of sizes and colors, determined at the time of packing. Exatouch not only allows them all to be managed under one UPC, but also allows the merchant to assign a local UPC to each variant, while still staying "connected" to the manufacturer's UPC. They can print the local barcode and manage each size-color as a unique UPC. If you're in retail, you get this!

Bulk

Bulk relationships are best explained with an example, like soda. A merchant may purchase soda by the case. However they may sell it by the case, a six-pack, or the can. Bulk management allows for a case to be removed from inventory and 4 six-packs to be put into inventory as a result. Or, a six-pack can be moved into six cans. A nice feature for convenience stores.

Vendor

Each Item is assigned vendors. So reordering is easy. The system knows which vender the PO goes to.

Alerts

Inventory levels are set to alert the merchant of low levels. Minimum order quantities are also settable.

Services

Exatouch allows services to be defined and sold on an order ticket as well. Of course there is no inventory for services per se, but the time and price is set, as well as the staff members who can perform the services. The optional Schedule feature allows for scheduling and check out to the register from the Schedule.

Customer Data

Complete contact information, birthday and referral information is managed in the POS system. Birthday emails based on customers' birthdays prove to be quite effective for marketing and getting the customer back into the store. The customer data also tracks purchase history which comes in handy for some businesses. Loyalty programs also track with customer data.

Purchasing

The purchasing module is a great way to ensure inventory cost efficiency and availability, both of which are true money-value features of a POS system like Exatouch.

Purchase Orders

Create POs for purchasing inventory items. POs can be printed or emailed to vendors.

Vendors

Vendors' contact information and items are tracked. The system knows which vendor(s) provide which products and building a PO makes smart use of this data. Each item is assigned a vendor(s).

Receiving

Receiving is easy and allows for label printing right on the spot. A nice feature of Exatouch receiving is the ability to receive a non-PO item. This happens frequently when a merchant visits a vendor and returns with a "special" purchase they did not anticipate. The Exatouch Receiver allows for creation of the special items at the time of receiving into inventory, including label printing.

Marketing

A number of marketing features are available with Exatouch.

- Email and automatic emails
- Text promotions
- Gift Certificates
- Gift Cards
- Loyalty
- Receipt Messages
- Customer Display message

Email marketing for example can cost hundreds per month from 3rd party providers,

Staff

The POS system by Exatouch keeps staff information like address, email, phone, and identification. The system goes further and tracks hire date, termination data, start rate, and hourly rate as well as commissions on items and services.

User Levels/Restrictions

Each staff member is assigned a 4 digit security pin for accessing the system. In addition, each user is assigned a User Type of either Administrator, Power User, or User. Each User Type comes with decreasing access rights.

Work Schedules

The system allows for creating and printing work schedules for each employee. A nice Exatouch feature is the ability to create a 2 week schedule to facilitate alternating weekly schedules, e.g. one weekend on, one weekend off.

Time Clock

A time clock is built-in for reporting time and attendance to a payroll system.

Reports

A full suite of reports are pre-built for easy recall by merchants. The reports provided are a result of user feedback and the Exatouch software team is always listening to users. Following is an example list of reports available.

Sales Reports

Each report can be generated for a particular date range.

- by Item,

- by SKU,

- by Categories,

- by Subcategory,

- by Staff,

- by Date,

- by Service,

- by Brand,

- by the three User Fields, etc.

There is also a

- settlement report for the merchant account,

- a transaction report highlighting transaction specific information,

- a sales tax summary,

- refund report,

- gift certificates, and a

- profit margin report.

Items Reports

- Items list sorted by Item, MFG, Category, Price.

- Service list sorted by Service, Description, Price, Duration

- An Inventory Value list.

Purchasing Reports

- Vendors List

- Vendor Items

- POs sorted by Number, Date, Vendor, Status.

Customer Reports

- Customer list by first name or last name

- Customer visit by date range.

Staff Reports

- Staff List

- Staff Services

- Time Clock by date range

- Time Details by Staff

- Staff Pay

- Staff Rollup

- Staff Bank Summary

- Staff Activity Log.

Scheduled Report Emails

A great feature for merchants is the schedule reporting sent via email. This feature allows the user to schedule up to twice daily reports to be sent to any email. As example, a store owner with two stores could schedule transaction reports to be sent every month to their accountant, and, sales reports twice a day to themselves.

Schedule

Schedule is a feature on Exatouch where the user can schedule services and check them out to the Register. The order built from the calendar can have items added to it. For example, a customer can be scheduled for an oil change, and then buy some cleaner products when they check out. The schedule is unusual in POS systems, but Exatouch has it. Nice functionality like double booking and adjusting and moving appointments make this a nice feature for businesses with services.

Messaging

The messaging feature allows for messages to customers or staff. This is a great marketing tool implemented right in the POS system. Promotions, like birthday specials, can be created and sent to customers … a great way to get them back into the store. Text promotions and email promotions are available.

Gift Certificates and Gift Cards

Exatouch has a unique feature called Programmable Gift Certificates. These certificates are implemented right in the system and act just like gift cards, but are simply printed on the receipt printer. When redeemed the balance is adjusted for future use, eliminating the need to refund or credit a portion.

In the cases where the store wants gift cards, they operate the same way, but the cards are available with logos/artwork to the merchant. Actually, as you are aware, gift cards are a good marketing tool as well ... they remind the customer of the business when they see the card.

Loyalty

Loyalty is an option in Exatouch. Here a customer loyalty program can be established where purchase history drives promotional value, or rewards, for the customers. This can be based on purchase amount or number of visits. After a milestone is met, an email can go out to the customer, and when they come in, they can redeem their reward.

SideKick™

SideKick is the name for an Exatouch system like a PADie running in tandem with another, for example an Atom. This allows the SideKick system to operate on the same data as the Atom system, or server. In this way a store can have a number of checkout machines. Better yet, a PADie SideKick is a great way to take the POS out onto the shop floor. The PADie

SideKick with available cordless barcode scanner is a great way to do inventory.

Direct Boarding – Exatouch does not use a gateway. ISOs who can board to an acquirer can do so directly as Exatouch is certified with First Data®, TSYS®, Vantiv®, EVO® Snap*, Mercury®, North American Bancard® Velocity, and Pivotal Payments FlexPoint™, with plans to certify to others.

A Gateway is essentially a server in the Cloud that receives payment transaction requests, forwards them to a payment acquirer, receives the response from the payment acquirer (e.g. approve/decline) and sends that response back to the payment application. Typically gateways charge fees and this will usually eat into the ISO's revenue and agent's residuals. This is not the case with solutions like Exatouch which are boarded directly to the processor and NOT through a gateway. iOS and Android tablet solutions all require a gateway and will therefore erode the revenue for ISOs and Agents.

Chapter 10 – Exatouch Products

Atom®

<u>Tightly integrated work station:</u>

Approximately iPad-size color touchscreen display, VFD customer facing display, 3" thermal printer, Card swiper, keyboard, 5-bill electronic cash drawer, Battery backup.

Optional: debit pin pad

PADie®

Exatouch FULL FEATURED small business software

NOT AN "APP"

Color touchscreen display

SQL Database Driven - NOT Cloud-only, but Cloud-Hybrid

USB Backup, your data is yours!

Optional: Cloud Backup

Full **POS Cash Register** with "button" input

Optional: Barcode scanner

Built-in **payment processing**

Optional: card swiper

Items and **Inventory**

Schedule and Sell **Services**

Email **reports**

Customer management

Staff management

Time clock

Purchasing/Vendor POs

PADie bundles include: a 3" thermal printer, card swiper, 5-bill electronic cash drawer

XT

<u>Traditional, yet modern component work station:</u>

15" color touchscreen display, VFD customer facing display, 3" thermal printer, Card swiper, keyboard, 5-bill electronic cash drawer, Battery backup.

Optional: debit pin pad

Go to Exatouch.com or call XTT for updated product information and details[2].

---

[2] Details and specifications subject to change.

Chapter 11 – Support

What can an ISO expect for support from a POS company? First and foremost you should expect a culture of support for your merchants. Unfortunately, some companies view support as a necessary evil, though that is not the norm.

More typical in POS will be fragmented support, just like the typical solution itself. When the software is from a different source than the hardware and the payment processing, the support is of course the same. POS is notorious for this type of user support experience; wrought with dissatisfaction.

Exatouch provides the hardware, software, and payment engine all nicely integrated and well supported. The company's culture is one of support by nature.

An all but overlooked component to POS support is ISO support. Exatouch takes ISO support very seriously, especially sales support. XTT knows that the ISO is our customer and the merchant is our user. Both layers of support experience are what stands out about Exatouch.

Sales support is evident in everything from demonstrations, to collateral material, and even an ISO-personalized web site.

The personalized website allows the ISO to use a link on their own website to link to the Exatouch.com website with only the ISO's contact information presented. The ISO can better sell to their POS merchants this way and be assured the contacts will go to them. This nice touch demonstrates XTT's commitment to the ISO.

Accessibility is key for support. Exatouch support, for example, is available via phone, on the web, in the software, on Facebook, Twitter, and even text messaging. This accessibility is true for both users and ISOs. Just another example of a true culture of support.

Like buying a car, you never really know how the service department is until you need them. However, kick the tires on your POS provider's support team. Call, text, email them and see what you get. That should illuminate what your merchant can expect as a user. Do they even have any ISO support?

As the consultant you want to become, be sure you can get the support YOU need as an ISO transitioning to POS.

Chapter 12 – Leasing

Leasing is a great way to provide a real POS system to your merchant while at the same time putting some extra money in your pocket with the deal; a true win-win. Partnering with a good leasing company can make the leasing process very easy. Note that it may be difficult to lease iPad and Android based solutions. Here's how leasing works:

First determine the complete cost of the system to the merchant. In examples like Exatouch, this may include a markup for you already … make note. Once you've determined the selling price for the system, this should be the amount they lease. Your leasing partner may give you Buy Rates and Sell Rates. The table below illustrates a Sell Rates table[3]. Depending on the merchant's credit and the term of the lease, you would multiply the factor in the table times the amount leased to find the payment. For example, using our example table below, a merchant with B credit leasing $2500 for 48 months should have a payment around: $2500 x .0325 = $78.

---

[3] The Sell Rate values provided here are provided for illustration purposes only.

The difference between your Buy Rates and your Sell Rates is called the "spread". To find the spread, calculate the deal using both your buy rates and sell rates and difference is the spread. The spread is another potential source of commission for you on the sale and one of the benefits of full point of sale technology solutions like Exatouch.

Sell Rates	12	24	36	48	60
P	.0980	.0510	.0370	.0300	.0250
A	.0980	.0520	.0380	.0315	.0270
B	.1040	.0535	.0400	.0325	.0295
C	.1160	.0570	.0420	.0340	.0320
D	.1370	.0590	.0500	.0430	.0390
E	.1580	.0630	.0590	.0530	.0560

Table 2 Leasing Illustration Sell Rates (will vary)

Leasing brings some requirements of you as the ISO or VAR agent. Once the lease is approved, the leasing company may fund some of the deal to get the equipment shipped. It is very likely they will not fund the entire deal until a Delivery and Acknowledgement (D&A) and/or a verbal confirmation are completed. The D&A is a form the merchant must sign and the verbal is a question and answer phone call the merchant must respond affirmatively to. This is important to be aware of as the process may delay your commissions.

Following are example questions that may be asked by the leasing company:

For security purposes what are the last four digits of your social security number? Please confirm your Date of Birth? Please confirm your business name and phone number? Did you sign the lease dated <date>? Do you agree that you signed a 5 page lease and received a copy of all pages of the lease? Do you agree that the lease has a term of 48 months, with monthly payment of $ 89 per month? Do you agree the lease is to finance an Exatouch POS System? Please confirm the serial number(s) and your MID? **Is your POS system installed and operating?** Do you understand that this lease will be paid through a direct debit bank account ending in: 1234? Are you aware that you have personally guaranteed this non-cancelable lease? Are you aware that we will collect taxes and fees and end of lease term options including the $150.00 restocking fee if exercising this option? Do you understand your lease will start immediately without any trial period?

Table 3 Example Lease Confirmation Questions

The confirmation should be straightforward if you've done a good job selling the POS to the merchant. They should be all eyes wide open. However, note question number 9. This can be a tricky question. Be sure to make the merchant aware that these questions are coming. Especially number 9. The script is the same script of questions leasing companies have used for standard credit card terminals. So, "Is your credit card terminal installed and operating?" is easy to answer since terminal really only transact. If they've seen a transaction, it's working.

However, point of sale systems are far more complex with many different functions. Answering the question "Is your POS system installed and operating?" may be an easy question to answer "I don't know to." If they answer anything but yes, the leasing company will likely not fund. Be sure to educate your POS merchant on the question. Let them know what "installed and operating" means: 1. they've seen a transaction, 2. they've seen a report, and 3. they've seen how to get help and support. Otherwise, they may honestly answer "I don't know" since it does so much they haven't seen, and, this will cause a delay in you getting paid.

Also be aware that merchant satisfaction is always important, especially during the first 60 days of the lease … this is the waiting period where the sales process is on the hook prior to the lease commitment kicking in. During this first 60 day waiting period, the merchant may have an easy time backing out of the lease if they are not happy; not necessarily, but discuss this with your leasing partner and be knowledgeable.

Chapter 13 – Future

EMV

EMV (Europay® MasterCard® and Visa®) is the platform for smart card, or, chip card payments. This card has an integrated circuit (IC) chip built-in that enables a more robust transaction handshake. The platform is defined by standards for the cards and the devices, protocols, and networks that read them. The US is anticipated to migrate to EMV capability in about 2015. As a new POS "consultant" stay informed about the impact of EMV and the ability of your POS partners to adapt. The primary impetus for EMV is as follows:

… the party, either the issuer or merchant, who does not support EMV, assumes liability for counterfeit card transactions.[4]

This means that the merchant must assure they support EMV transactions if they don't want to assume liability for counterfeit cards they accept. EMV will require a POS that supports chip cards. Of particular concern is the impact EMV will have on iPad POS and other App POS products. The implementation and cost of an EMV card device alone is contrary to the iPad POS model. It is very likely iPad and

---

[4] *EMV FOR U.S. ACQUIRERS: SEVEN GUIDING PRINCIPLES FOR EMV READINESS*, Miller, Berg, Stroud, Paese; MasterCard Advisors

Android POS solutions being sold today will have to be replaced in order to support EMV. EMVCo.com is one source of information on EMV as are Visa and MasterCard.

Exatouch is well positioned to enable EMV in its products and plans to do so much sooner than 2015. Stay tuned. For example, Exatouch is already interfaced to a number of EMV devices and will be EMV-ready when the device's EMV software kernels are released.

Merchant Ecosystem and Future-proofing

Exatouch is the core of a merchant ecosystem that will bring small retailers technology only available to large retail, and more. There is a whole ecosystem of software and hardware, in-store, Cloud, and social technologies that small retail can benefit, and ISOs can profit, from. At the heart of this core is payment processing, which almost disappears from the conversation, but is the heart nonetheless. That ecosystem is the future of the payments industry with mobile, marketing, social, beneficial, affinity, security, service, and communications spokes all centralized on the payment hub and POS. Be sure your POS partner shares this vision with you for your merchant clients and they will be yours for a long, long time.

Chapter 14 – Pricing

Following is an example table showing Exatouch ISO pricing for the Atom Classic™ as of publication[5]. Contact your Exatouch representative for updated and complete pricing or visit Exatouch.com.

System	$1,995
Software	included
Swiper	included
Cash Drawer	included
Keyboard	included
Receipt Printer	included
Stand	included
Barcode Scanner	$179
Support for 48 mos.	$899
Customer Display	included
Total 48 mo. Cost:	**$3,073**

---

[5] Pricing is subject to change without notice. Contact XTT for current ISO pricing.

Chapter 15 – Competing Products

There are a good number of POS choices out there. From iPad apps and traditional component systems to patchwork DIY, the ISO agent should be familiar with the various choices and how to guide their merchants to the best choice. Here are a few examples:

Cloud, App, iPad, and Android

As tech guys, we love our Android phones, our iPads, the Cloud, and apps. It's all fun stuff that can be quite useful and not just entertaining. Mobile payments on this technology is a great addition to our market and will prove to be for a long time. However mobile transactions are a far cry from full-featured POS.

Let's call the light version of POS offered on this technology "App POS". App POS will have a place in the market too. However, an iPad didn't replace your home computer and it won't likely replace a business computer any time soon. That said, tablet solutions can be valuable as a component to a retail system. This means either in-store mobility or in-field mobility with a data connection to the business. Exatouch PADie$^{®}$ operates in SideKick™ mode out on the floor for transactions, look-up, and taking inventory. However, it is a full functioning POS device, not just an app.

Below are some details and pros and cons of App POS.

iPad®s and Android® Tablets

Examples are: ShopKeep®, Lavu® POS, Clover®, NCR® Silver™, Revel®, and Leaf®. All have similar cost models: equipment cost plus app fee.

Example Cost

	ShopKeep®
iPad®	$399
App Fee	$2,352
Swiper	$149
Cash Drawer	$139
Keyboard	$69
Receipt Printer	$299
Stand	$120
Barcode Scanner	$399
Customer Display	NOT AVAILABLE
Total 48 mo. Cost:	**$3,926**

Pros

Sexy – There is an almost religious following for Apple products. The iPad is a sexy toy and great for photos, music, browsing, and entertaining apps. Samsung's and others' Android tablets have all but surpassed the iPad so, ditto for Android tabs.

Handy – iPads and other tablets are handy; small, light, easy to carry.

Convenient – Many merchants already have an iPad or other entertainment tablet. However, they may not want to "sacrifice" it for their business and will have to buy another.

Familiar – By now many people are familiar with iPads and Android.

Cloud-based – the data processing and reporting that is available via an app can be accessed from anywhere the app is connected to the Internet, or from a PC on the Internet, if part of the authorized service.

Cons

Residuals – App POS typically threatens processing revenue and many times will board a merchant if they can. This leaves ISO accounts exposed revenue sharing.

Gateway – Must run via a gateway like USAePay®, and therefore compete with ISOs for processing revenue.

Not PCI – iPad and Android apps are ineligible for PCI PA-DSS validation for secure transactions, and therefor are NOT PCI compliant. Despite surprising success with claims that a gateway's PCI-DSS server site compliance somehow translates to a merchant's business site, this is not the case. PCI further calls for any payment application (PA) regardless of gateway approvals, encryption, or otherwise to be PA-DSS validated. As of this writing there are no iPad or Android based POS apps that are PCI validated.

Not Full POS – App POS is just that, an app. Many of the features like full customer management, full inventory control, email marketing, reporting, data export to accounting, mixed payments types, gift certificates, etc. don't exist or must be handled through a computer and the Cloud.

Many merchants and business owners find the restricted usability uncomfortable.

Theft – Tablet POS is known to be theft-prone. iPads and tablets are attractive to many users for obvious reasons and they do disappear from stores too frequently.

Data in the Cloud – Business-critical data is not in the store, it is in the Cloud. If the merchant decides to cancel the app service, they can end up with none of their data, unlike full POS where the data is in the store, and on USB back up or even Cloud backup.

Clunky – Piecing together the components for POS running on an iPad can be daunting for many small retailers. There is no USB so barcode scanners, cash drawers, and printers are all expensive network and wireless devices.

Expensive – Despite the first appearance as inexpensive, iPad-based POS is actually quite expensive. The monthly app fee makes the total cost of ownership for the business owner quite high. Peripherals like scanner and cash drawer are expensive.

Light Duty – iPads are not full function computers. They run on a special kind of microprocessor chip called and "embedded processor". These processors are application-specific chips for cars, cable TV boxes, smartphones, and iPods, etc. Computing and data processing capability will always be limited. This is why they must run on the Cloud, held up by proper computers up there.

No USB – There is no USB port on iPads. Only a proprietary port and cable. So backup and other peripherals are Apple-expensive and a whole lot less convenient.

Finicky – It's well documented that iPads in commercial applications are known to be finicky. That means that the network connection and peripherals are unstable. The result is extreme discomfort for the store personnel in the middle of a transaction with a failed connection. Printing is a known source of merchant frustration.

Cloud Only – Lack of processing power and memory forces iPads and Android tablets to operate "in the Cloud". This means they are merely an access device that uses the Internet to transact and data-process through web servers.

When the Internet connection goes down (like that never happens?!) you're dead in the water. Not just for transactions, which isn't that bad, but NO DATA either. Buyer beware.

Temperature Forced Shut Down – If an iPad ever reaches a certain internal temperature, it will shut down. So if you leave it in the sunlight of a window in the store, be advised it could shut down.

pcAmerica

Example Cost

System	$2,695
Software	$899
Swiper	incl
Cash Drawer	incl
Keyboard	incl
Receipt Printer	incl
Stand	incl
Barcode Scanner	$179
Support for 48 mos.	$3,312
Customer Display	incl
Total 48 mo. Cost:	**$7,085**

pcAmerica® (PCA) by Automation, Inc. is a long standing member of the POS market since 1985. With thousands of installations, PCA has partnered with many POS dealers.

PCA for retail is called Cash Register Express™ and their restaurant version is Restaurant Pro Express™. PCA is a software-only product. The company offers bundled hardware from 3rd parties like Dell™, Elo®, Toshiba, and HP.

PCA software is licensed and supported apart from the hardware it runs on.

Pros

<u>Full POS</u> – Being a full software POS application, these products have a full set of POS features.

<u>Well-Established</u> – PCA has been around a long time.

<u>In-store Data</u> – Runs on a local database, not in the Cloud.

<u>Available to ISOs</u> – PCA is available to ISOs, usually through a 3rd party value added reseller (VAR) for bundling with hardware.

<u>Residuals</u> – PCA does not typically share in processing revenue though some VARs may want to.

<u>PA-DSS</u> – PCA is on the PCI PA-DSS validation list.

Cons

<u>Cost</u> – Relatively speaking, PCA is on the high-end for total cost of ownership.

<u>Not-integrated</u> – The system is a non-integrated solution, requiring component hook ups.

<u>Not very sexy</u> – Very much a traditional, though tried and true, form factor for point of sale.

<u>Support</u> – In most cases software support and hardware support are from two different sources, often outsourced and potentially non-domestic.

Harbortouch

Example Cost:

System	incl
Software	incl
Swiper	incl
Cash Drawer	incl
Keyboard	incl
Receipt Printer	incl
Stand	incl
Barcode Scanner	incl
Support for 48 mos.	$5,232
Customer Display	incl
Total 48 mo. Cost:	**$5,232**

Harbortouch is the name for United Bancard's POS offering, and in fact is their DBA. United Bancard® is a super ISO with many ISO entities and agent under their umbrella. They have thousands of merchants. Harbortouch is only available to Harbortouch ISOs and agents.

Pros

<u>Low up-front</u> – there is a low initial out of pocket cost. The monthly support fee is more like a nothing-down rent payment.

<u>Large company</u> – One of the first movers for POS from an ISO.

<u>One Support Call</u> – Harbortouch provides the software, hardware, and merchant account, so support is from one company.

<u>Traditional</u> – Harbortouch is a traditional form factor POS system so it's familiar, tried and true.

Cons

<u>Rent-like</u> – the merchant doesn't own the system, the support payment is akin to a rent payment where at the end of a contract, the equipment still belongs to Harbortouch.

<u>An ISO</u> – Harbortouch is an ISO. They only provide POS via their ISOs and agents. Therefore, they only share a portion of the processing revenue.

<u>Their account</u> – Any merchant account associated with a Harbortouch POS system belongs to Harbortouch.

<u>Cost</u> – On the high side of the market for total cost of ownership (actually not owned).

Patchwork

One alternative some businesses may opt for is to piece together their own system by purchasing POS hardware and software separately on their own, perhaps on line. Some level of success may be attainable for the tech savvy owner, but this is more likely to result in frustration and dissatisfaction at a minimum. The impression of cost saving going the patchwork route is a false one. By the time you factor in the all the components required, including the payment software and time, this alternative should be less and less interesting. In fact, over a 48 month period, a patchwork solution stands the risk of costing more than most.

Tight integration of a system like Exatouch with support and ISO involvement should make selling around a patchwork solution very easy for most busy merchants.

Chapter 16 – Batch Out

We hope you now have a quiver full of arrows for attacking your POS transition. From the why, the what, to the how, you should now be armed with a good base of POS knowledge.

An approach for sales and a lead program, messaging to work with, benefits of POS, a good run down of POS features to sell, overcoming objections, PCI, apps, Cloud, product comparisons ... the ISO and ISO agents can now kick-off an effective program with all this information provided.

Don't forget the why, the 5 Rs. Your ISO business is changing and your future likely depends on POS. "Settle" ;^) on a good POS solution and partner and make it happen!

Index

Notes

www.ingramcontent.com/pod-product-compliance
Lightning Source LLC
Chambersburg PA
CBHW060637210326
41520CB00010B/1646